Prelude

In 1973, I unwittingly fell into an adventure.

I discovered an old-looking book with a burlap binding. It was Thomas Merton's *Seeds of Contemplation*. Merton was a Trappist monk who studied "Eastern Mysticism", meditation, and collaborated with Zen Buddhist monks on the spiritual path of meditation.

Intrigued and eager, I started meditating. That was the moment I started a life-long adventure - I now know it is an adventure into awareness. I discovered a presence, and my own heart became aware of what it means to be human. While sidetracked many times by the busyness of life, family, and career, I have adapted my meditations to meet the needs of the moment.

Now, after deepening my practice and reading the science of meditation and quantum physics, I share my thoughts and poetry with others.

I'm inviting you into a conversation as a co-adventurer. Enjoy the journey!

Contents

To my Soulmate, Barbara

A human being is a part of the whole, called by us "Universe," a part limited in time and space. He experiences himself, his thoughts and feelings as something separate from the rest — a kind of optical delusion of his consciousness. The striving to free oneself from this delusion is the one issue of true religion. Not to nourish it but to try to overcome it is the way to reach the attainable measure of peace of mind.

Albert Einstein, 1950

Introduction

As I was putting this collection together, I naturally asked my Soulmate, Barbara, to pre-read, comment and provide other types of feedback (I was especially concerned about my undisciplined sketches).

She wrote this lovely note:

"You have inner peace.
If only you'd let go of past judgements.
If only you'd ignore present judgements.
And flow in the now
No judgements."

How incredibly insightful is that? That is really the heart of the spiritual adventure. Letting go of your judgments, transcending the self. Just let go.

As spiritual beings we are on a journey to transcend Einstein's "optical delusion," accept our Oneness and live into our place in the Universe.

What better time than now for us to free ourselves from our delusion and awaken to our oneness -

**With each other
With the world around us
With the universe**

**So we can live with hearts of compassion
in mutual understanding & peace.**

*Out beyond ideas of wrongdoing and right-doing,
there is a field.
I will meet you there.
When the soul lies down in that grass, the world is too
full to talk about. Words, language, even the idea of
"each other" has lost meaning.
- Rumi*

Part I

**An Adventure
into Awareness & Presence**

J.R.R. Tolkien was a master storyteller. His *Hobbit* and *Lord of the Rings* are grand adventures. The hobbits in both adventures weren't looking for an adventure at all - and were very reluctant as they set out on the adventure, unsure of what it would bring. There were many good times and bad times in the adventure, with odd characters and many dangers. At the end of the adventure was a grand goal.

So it is, in a way, with our spiritual adventure. We aren't really sure at the beginning what we are getting ourselves into. We may be very reluctant to look outside of the solipsistic fugue we are trapped in - Einstein's optical delusion. This delusion is very comfortable, and we've lived there our whole life. In fact, we may be absolutely certain that our little home is real, and that nothing exists outside of it.

Step outside. The starting point is meditation.

As we develop our meditation practice, we learn to quiet our default mode network (or our "ego," our local self) and make space between our thoughts, our  emotions. As we settle into that space, we settle into open awareness. We can be openly aware of our thoughts, our emotions, the sounds and energy of the world in which we live.

1973, Altamont NY

In the fall of 1973 I was attending a college seminary in Altamont, NY, just a short way from Albany. The college was halfway up a mountain that formed the Heidelberg Escarpment and the beginning of the Adirondack Mountains.

It was a beautiful setting. In the fall, I loved hiking in the woods up the mountain to a spot we called "High Point" at the top of the escarpment. So beautiful and peaceful.

But the winter of 1973-74 was very bitter. The wind whipped up and down the mountain, and there was a lot of snow. It was the height of the 1973 Arab Oil Embargo. Heating oil - and the heat our boiler produced - was a precious commodity.

The wind blew so hard that winter snow came through the old windows and piled up on the windowsills.

This was the setting for my introduction to meditation. Our library was carpeted and had radiant heat in the floor. It was the warmest room in the building.

So, I spent a lot of time in the library.
On the floor.
Between the book stacks.
Sleeping.
I was such a serious student!

As I woke from a nap one day, I had a chance encounter. I looked up and saw this curious old book with burlap binding. I pulled it out of the shelf, and it was Thomas Merton's *Seeds of Contemplation*. Merton was a Trappist monk who studied Eastern religions, mysticism and meditation. He died in 1968 in Thailand while attending a monastic conference with Zen Buddhist monks. Not so much anymore - but in 1968 Merton was a controversial figure.

Since I loved controversy, I read the book. And I started meditating.

And so, the winter of 1973-74 went on.

In the early spring, I went for a walk one afternoon.

The ground was still very wet and there were patches of snow in the shade of the forest. It was muddy on the path. I hiked up to High Point, overlooking Altamont and the Hudson Valley. It was a clear, sunny afternoon. In the distance across the valley there was a hazy line of mountains.

I sat there, cross-legged on the stone bluff, and started my meditation.

What happened next, I can't describe completely - words don't do it. It was like time stopped. Reality shifted. The scene stretched out before me came alive and melted together like honey. Still distinct, but somehow one. All questions faded away. Nothing mattered anymore. It was just this . . . field of awareness that was floating through everything.

No clue. I don't know how long I sat there. It could have been seconds or minutes. Certainly not hours because it didn't get dark. But then, it didn't really matter. Time did not exist, and everything was one. Flowing. Becoming. It was like I had awoken to a new reality.

As a college student studying philosophy, I was very ill prepared to understand what was happening. I was perplexed and worried about what happened - it was so out of context with everything I knew and thought. I kept meditating, and the experiences continued.

In a cemetery in Ingram, Texas.

Out on the ice on Stuart Lake in Michigan.

Sitting on a bench by an old Norman castle in Aghadoe, Ireland.

Watching a sheep in Kingsbarns, Scotland.

And in my study on my meditation cushion.

The Science of Meditation

So, what happens when we meditate? Meditation can be (and is) a spiritual practice. It is also a very natural practice that has many benefits for our physical, emotional and mental health. The experiences of meditation have a very sound basis in science and medicine.

There are two key neural networks when

we meditate: our autonomic nervous system and our default mode network.

Autonomic Nervous System

The autonomic nervous system is the brain's connection through our brain stem to our body's critical systems, and the external world. This is how our body regulates itself at all levels - all under the radar of our conscious thoughts. There are two primary states of our nervous system:

- Sympathetic state: prepare for fight or flight, or freeze. It's our survival response when we are in danger.

- Parasympathetic state: controls our body during normal circumstances. It's safe to eat, connect, reproduce and sleep.

Here is a fun fact: If we see a child with a face contorted in pain and hear a shrieking scream, our amygdala reacts within 300 milliseconds. Hormones are released, our heart rate and breathe rate elevate. Our body is preparing for fight or flight - to spring into action, long before we have a chance to "think." So, why is this in a discussion about meditation? The autonomic nervous system is critically important to our evolution and continued survival. While normal operation is all under the radar of our conscious thought, our conscious thought can impact the state of our nervous system. If we are in a constant state of stress or distress - our mind continues to run patterns of thought about past events, traumas, emotions and worries about the future - we can get caught in a state of rigidity. Our "normal" state can be in a sympathetic state.

We can also interrupt the conditions that put us into a sympathetic state and shift gears into a parasympathetic state through conscious thoughts and actions.

Let's do a quick exercise.

Sit comfortably in our chairs, close our eyes. Soften our faces into a slight smile. Take three deep, cleansing breaths. Breathe deeply in through our nose, into our diaphragm. Exhale slowly, sighing out of our mouth.

Let's do it now. When we finish the third

cleansing breath, we will slowly open our eyes.

Breathe

Breathe

Breathe

What did we feel? Waves of relaxation flow through our body. Almost like a soft energy pulse. We have started to signal our body that we are safe. Did our heart rate variability improve, our heart and breath rates slow? We are freeing our self to be connected and loving. Our brain and body no longer need to focus on danger, fight or flight.

Default Mode Network

Marcus Raichle is a neuroscientist at Washington University in St. Louis. In the 1990's into 2001, he was doing research on changes in brain activity, blood flow and oxygen consumption using functional magnetic resonance imaging (fMRI). He was monitoring brain activity when it did a complex task - counting backward from 1,475 by 13. It takes a lot of focus! He made an interesting discovery: When the brain was focused on a complex task, specific areas of the brain went "quiet" or dark. Oddly enough, when the brain was doing "nothing" those same areas lit up. These areas were the midline prefrontal cortex and the post cingula cortex, which connects to the limbic system. When research subjects were asked what they were thinking of during this time, they said their minds were wandering, thinking of the past, feelings, memories, plans, etc.

This became known as the "Default Mode Network" - what our brain does when there is nothing for it to do. In default mode, the mind wanders and focuses on everything about "me":

> How am I doing?
> How do I feel?
> What happened to me in the past?
> What am I going to do in the future?
> Who do I love (or hate)?

This is where our brain builds the sense of "me", our sense of self. Our ego.

The autonomic nervous system and our default mode network are our friends. They are critical to our health and survival. However, when we get caught in a place of rigidity, we see everything through the lens of "me." Or we get caught in a place of trauma . . . Or we get overwhelmed in a constant state of stress or emotion.

We are now caught in Einstein's optical delusion . . . living in the hell of our solipsistic fugue.

Altered State

Meditation is a release from this default. We create a relaxed, parasympathetic state. We are safe, solid and positive. With our focused attention on our breath, we are quieting the mind - soothing the default mode network. In this state, we see and observe our thoughts - as an observer rather than an inquisitor, free from judgement.

We now can be aware of the world as it actually is. We become present to now - the ultimate dimension. In open awareness and presence, our concept of time slips away.

We have now freed ourselves from our mental constructs and narratives about reality, and are free to experience it in the moment, as it really is, not how we think of it.

The reality we encounter is beautiful, abundant and multi-dimensional. We have now entered into an "altered state." It is incredibly different from the world our default mode network plays in . . .

In his book, *Mind - A Journey to the Heart of Being Human*, Dan Siegel discusses the "Decade of the Mind," the 1990s. During that time a multi-disciplined group of scientists (neuroscientists, neurobiologists, psychologists, sociologists, physicists) and philosophers collaborated on an investigation of what the "Mind" is. The real question was: Is the mind just the result of neurosynaptic firings in the brain, or was it something beyond that?

Neuroscientists had developed the theory of neuroplasticity - the ability of the brain to continue developing throughout life by re-wiring itself. But was that it? Was the mind just the result of electrochemical reactions and connections in the brain? And when the brain stopped, that's it? The mind is caput?

A whole bunch of smart people came up with this working definition of the mind: The flow and organizing of information/ energy. The implication of this is mind-boggling. Our mind, then, extends out beyond our brain - into our body through the autonomic nervous system. And it extends further - as we experience phenomena through our eyes, our ears, our nose, our mouth and our touch - our mind extends out beyond our body into the world we experience and the people/beings with which we interact.

In this adventure into awareness and presence, we transcend our local "self" and free ourselves into oneness with everyone on the planet, all beings and the world around us. Our hearts open to the oneness and grow in compassion and love. Our mind opens to mutual understanding. Not only do we feel peaceful - we become peace. Our very presence in the world is a powerful source of compassion, love & peace.

As we dwell in this oneness, we also transcend our local world.

We become one with the nonlocal - that which not only spans all of spacetime, but eternally and infinitely transcends spacetime itself. We have awoken. We are liberated. We are as we always were - we had no journey to get there.

We are in heaven.

Part II

**Poems, Musings
& Meditations**

deep, dark mist
covers the rotted tree
and speaks of primeval surging
long, long past
returned as of late
at last
at long, long last

unravel the moment
and discover eternity

every moment is the moment of the
burning bush
the moment of breath - my peace i give to you
the moment of love
the moment of pain
the moment of birth
the moment of death
becoming, ending
the mountain moves and the mountain
stays
the moment of eternity

here
now

everything that ever was
everything that is now
everything that ever shall be

is

as it was then
is now
and ever shall be

all is one
and the same

everything that is
is
as it is . . .

"*People like us, who believe in physics, know that the distinction made between past, present and future is nothing more than a persistent, stubborn illusion*"

- Albert Einstein

an angel looked down on me
held me in her tight embrace
face of ecstasy
sweet breath of honey
reached deep
deep into me
touched my heart
and pulled out my soul

"For a hypothetically super-sensible being, there would be no 'flowing' of time: the universe would be a single block of past, present and future"

- Carlo Rovelli

i move the pen
very slowly
ink flows onto the page
bell rings, gentle breeze
time stops
frozen blackberries
eternity arrives
chirp --

"Reality is not what you think it is."

- Me

frozen blueberries
here we go again
and again
eternity comes rushing
out of the eye of a needle

tiny bugs, little flies
jumped on the old screen
fresh lake breeze
summer sounds
the watcher watched
little elbows on the table

the watcher watched
and wondered

church bell rings
a lonely sound
sharp and clear
in the cold winter air

a casket rolls slowly
down the walk
in another world a car
drives by

how odd
don't they know
life has stopped?

"And the day was going on in the college just as if he were there."

- James Joyce, A Portrait of the Artist as a Young Man

the butterfly flapped its wings
in china

no wait

the butterfly is flapping its wings

ok

the butterfly is going to flap its wings

don't mind me

i'm going to enjoy the butterfly
flapping its wings

if dollars were daisies
i'd wear them on my belt

what?

50 years

finally –

and the dirt was so moist
you would think there'd be worms

but none

"Look at the birds in the sky . . ."
- Matthew 6:26

i am the butterfly
flapping its wings
i am the seraphim
in the heavens
i am the doodle bug

we are as we always were
in the endless
song and dance

going nowhere
being everywhere

the watcher watched
and wondered

and the garbage truck roared by

i am a cork
floating in the endless ocean
washed gently
in the waves of time
ocean of eternity
washing in
on the shores of humanity

Eternity

pitter patter
raindrops fall
knocking gently
announcing the moment
of eternity

that day on high point
so many years ago
it's been 42 years
and i still cannot find the words
to describe it
or express the experience

and yet it is with me constantly

the trees were there

have you ever listened
to the drumbeat of the snow?
the gentle tapping
as each flake falls
and kisses the snowpack so soft
out in the silence
the frozen expanse
the drumbeat of the snow

come

listen to the gentle song of reality
the softly hummed melody
that binds us all
listen to the gentle song of reality
the hills and the mountains
will add their deep chant
the clear lakes and rivers
the soft refrain
the snowflakes gentle touch as they fall
and the pitter patter of the dropping rain

come

listen to the gentle song of reality
as it ebbs and flows with time
singing into eternity

listen to the song of reality
to the melody of eternity
in it a quiet voice speaks

horribly mundane
terribly normal
every day
every moment
right here

now is the moment
we've all be waiting for
we are the ones
been looking for

the trees were there
and they know
they gently whisper
and speak to me
from time to time

and the hills

that which has been seen
cannot be described
that which has been heard
cannot be discussed

perhaps it cannot be spoken, only heard
perhaps it cannot be conceived only felt

or maybe not

now at this moment

here at this place

and eternity rushed out through the eye
of the needle

what?

the watcher watched and wondered
who is the watcher
and what is really going on?

here

now

i am lost
and
i am home
i am wandering in the desert
i am laying in the grassy field

the banshee came
i sat and listened to its shriek

the banshee came
the shrieking stopped

i sat and listened to the silence
and the peace

i am stepping outside of time
the relentless march
all that i once knew fading
and becoming
that which i do not yet know

**i am
one aware
of one
who is**

"Entanglement arises because there is only one wave function for the entire universe, not separate wave functions for each piece of it"

- Sean Carroll, Something Deeply Hidden

someday my love
i will tell you a wonderful secret
not now
some other now
we will know the time
i will whisper the secret
gently into your heart
our souls are one
fulfilled in eternity

wake up now
we are here
we have arrived
where we never left
and always were
wake up now
and be here

how long?
stepping out of time -
that relentless march
of what i once knew
to that which i do not yet know
when you let go of time
it gets weird
there is only now
and its flow

i am, however
very curious
about what might be next

the trees are here
and they gently whisper
and the hills
the walls
the world of reality around me
they gently whisper
as i enter the garden of nothingness
and float on the waves of time
gently into my soul they whisper
and inform me
as i sit on my cushion rooted deeply
the bell rings
time stops
my eyes open

now what?

the shift
from trying to control reality
to loving reality
as it is

a deep, dark winter
has covered my heart
i sit here in hope
love and compassion
waiting for the birth of spring

when you dive deeply
into the pool of now
you find yourself
bathed in the refreshing waters
of eternity

eternity comes rushing out
of the eye of a needle

chirp -

there only is
and all that is
is one

i am one
aware
of one who is

we are one
aware
of one who are

i pray father
that we may be one
just as you and he are one

the final dissolution of self
into the eternal now
oneness
the kingdom of god

the trees were there,
and they know
they speak to me of it
from time to time
in the gentle whisper of their being

my mind is open
to the present moment
release and be still

my heart is open
to the present moment
release and feel the stillness

listen to the stillness
feel the eternal

i am open
i am free
i am peace

here i am
what am i going to do?
how do i respond

i have a choice

i have an open mind
a loving heart
aware of the endless possibilities

i am where i'm supposed to be
doing what i'm supposed to do
on my soul purpose

here
now

our understanding is limited
by our human experience
our experience is limited
by our human understanding

something is going on
and i'm not sure what it is

the watcher watched
and wondered

all that i ever was
all that i ever will be
i am now

breathing in
breathing out

my breath is the breath of christ
breathing in with jesus
breathing out my peace i give to you

my eyes are the eyes of christ
breathing in with jesus
breathing out my eyes smile
on all people with loving kindness

my words are the words of christ
breathing in with jesus
breathing out speaking words of love
words of compassion
words of understanding
words of peace
my words uplift and comfort

breathing in with jesus
breathing out
my peace i give to you

each thought, each word has energy
and ripples out into the world around me

i can choose the ripples i create

mutual understanding, love and peace

or

misunderstanding, fear and violence

i choose mutual understanding
love
and peace

each moment i am confronted with a
choice

the way of fear,
misunderstanding,
anger,
hate
war

or

the way of love
compassion
mutual understanding
peace

may all that i think, say and do
be expressions of
love
compassion
understanding
peace

i greet this moment
as an awaken soul
i vow to live each moment deeply
and smile on all beings with the eyes of
compassion

Part III

The Meditation Challenge

"His soul had arisen from the grave of boyhood, spurning her graveclothes. Yes! Yes! Yes! He would create proudly out of the freedom and power of his soul as the great artificer whose name he bore, a living thing, new and soaring and beautiful, impalpable, imperishable"

- James Joyce, A Portrait of the Artist as a Young Man

The Benefits of Meditation

30 years of evidence supports the benefits of meditation.

Experienced meditators know that meditation creates an altered state, a sense of wellbeing, peace, love. Perception of yourself, others and reality begin to shift in this altered state. The million-dollar question taken up by Daniel Goleman and Richard Davidson in their book, *Altered Traits*, is this: Can repeated meditation and exposure to these altered states create scientifically measured changes in our brain and body?

The answer is yes. Meditation does produce scientifically measurable changes in our bodies and in society.

Just to summarize a few:

- There is a correlation between the perceived stress scores of participants in meditation training and the density of their amygdala. The amygdala is a key player in the fight or flight response.

- After mindfulness training, subjects showed a change in hippocampal grey matter. The hippocampus houses our short- and long-term memory.

• After eight weeks of mindfulness-based stress reduction training, Lazar Labs at Harvard noted changes in meditators vs control groups. Areas of the brain impacted were the posterior cingulate cortex, cerebellum, temporo-parietal junction and hippocampus.

• As we age, we lose cortical thickness in our brain. Again, from Lazar Labs, the loss of cortical thickness is less in meditators as they age.

• Fluid intelligence is our capacity to think logically and solve problems in novel situations. Not surprising, fluid intelligence declines as we age. Unless you are a meditator or yogi.

• Telomeres are DNA material that cap the ends of chromosomes in our cells. As cells divide, these telomeres become shorter . . . this is a process called cellular aging. Eventually the cell can no longer reproduce properly, or cell division ends. A handful of research shows that meditation can slow down the process (and maybe even reverse) and help improve our overall health span . . . that part of our life when we are healthy.

What does all this mean? The effects and benefits of meditation are real and have real impact on our brain and body. We used to think that when a baby was born, its brain continued to develop through adolescence into young adulthood. And then it was finished. Now, however, scientists have documented that in fact our brain continues to develop and change throughout life.

Our brains consist of about 86 billion neurons - specialized cells that communicate with each other using electrical and chemical signals. As they communicate, they form neuro circuits or pathways. Through a process called neuroplasticity, our brain can actually form new neural circuits. As Dan Seigel points out, the basic principle is: "Where neurons flow, connections grow." In essence, the brain can "rewire" itself through repeated activity.

As we meditate, we are entering into a state of open awareness and presence. The attributes of this state are connectedness, compassion, love and peace. The more we enter into this state, we are rewiring our brains. As we rewire our brains, we now are making these states into real traits, and we carry them into our normal, everyday life. With persistence, our everyday life becomes a meditation, and the change in our selves leaks out into society and the world around us.

I love this quote from Richard Davidson, one of the authors of Altered Traits. He was being interviewed by Krista Tippett on an On Being podcast titled, *A Neuroscientist on Love and Learning* (February 14, 2019).

"When humans came on this planet, we didn't evolve and immediately start brushing our teeth. We all brush our teeth several times a day.

"We envision a time when we will recognize that our minds are just as important as our teeth. Doing a simple mental exercise, I think, will be recognized as a really urgent public health need."

Discovery of Self

"Troublez l'eau: vous y voyez-vous?
Laissez-la reposer
Vous verrez alors votre image."
- Jean de La Fontaine

I fell in love with this quote the first time I heard it in 1974. The story is from one of La Fontaine's fables. It's about three saints who are having a conversation about self-discovery. The older of the three tells them to look at a pool of water as he stirs up the water. "What do you see there?" He continues, "Let the water be still, and you will see your face."

This is where meditation starts: Be still. As we sit in stillness, we begin to see our self. We observe our bodily sensations, our emotions and our thoughts. We let them be present and accept them as they are. This fosters a deeply intimate awareness of our self.

Dan Seigel has a beautiful meditation called the *Wheel of Awareness* (danseigel.com).

In the meditation he walks us through our awareness in five areas of our self:
 • awareness of our senses

- awareness of our body
- awareness of our thoughts and emotions
- awareness of our awareness
- awareness of our intention of loving kindness for all people

With this meditation, Dr. Seigel walks us through differentiating the aspects of our self - and as we get to awareness of our awareness, we realize we aren't only our sense, we aren't only our bodily sensations, we are't only our thoughts and emotions. There is a central core of awareness that floats in and out of all our self.

As we move into the final stage of the meditation, loving kindness for our self and others, we begin to blossom into a new awareness: We live in an interconnected, interdependent world. This frees us into a real sense of love and compassion for all beings. We are no longer as interested in trying to control reality as we are in love with reality as it is.

Our adventure has taken us through discovery of our self and into discovery of the true Self - the oneness that binds us all.

The Wandering Mind

One of the biggest barriers to meditation that I hear from folks is, "I just can't quiet my mind!"

In his book, *Bliss Brain*, Dawson Church discusses the four stages of meditation:

- Focused Awareness
- Mind Wandering
- Realization
- Shift

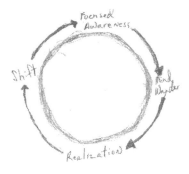

Focused Awareness is what everyone thinks meditation is. However, meditation is actually the full cycle of what happens when we meditate. Focused awareness is that state of open awareness and presence when we are focused on our meditation. It can be our breath, a guided meditation, our steps, sounds. Our default mode network quiets and we are at peace. Highly experienced meditators like monks and yogis with over 10,000 hours of meditation can sustain this period of meditation for long periods of time.

The rest of us are not so highly trained. Eventually, maybe after a few seconds or minutes, our minds wander off. This is very natural and shouldn't discourage us. This is just the mind doing what the mind does. It slips into its default mode.

If we stick with our meditation, we realize that our mind has wandered. This is the important part. When I realize that my mind has wandered, I like to bring a soft smile to my face and have gratitude for my mind. Maybe a little bit of mirth that my mind has done it again. It's very natural.

And then we shift our focus back. We let the thoughts or emotions float off like a puffy cloud in the sky and return to our open awareness.

It is very important that we treat our self with compassion. This is what our minds very naturally do. There is no reason to get frustrated or give up.

Remember, neuroscientists have proven neuroplasticity - the ability of the brain to rewire itself. The more we practice meditation, the easier it is for us to quiet the mind and spend more time in that peaceful state of open awareness and presence.

Keep in mind that even experienced meditators have minds that wander - sometimes more than others. I've been meditating in some form since 1973 and there are days that my mind won't quiet and I find it difficult to complete an entire meditation session.

The Real Treasure

The real treasure of the meditation adventure is this: As we persist in our meditation practice and develop our ability to quiet our mind, the state of open awareness and presence begins to extend into the rest of our life - the times when we are not "meditating." The inner calm becomes part of us. As we go through our daily life and all of its tribulations, it is there as a resource for us.

Not only do we have an inner calm, we also become connected with each other and the world around us, and are aware of the interdependence of all beings. This opens us for compassion and love. We are now in the proverbial "state of grace."

Action Steps

So, there are some simple things we can do to start a meditation practice or if we are going through a period when it's difficult to quiet the mind.

Firstly, keep in mind that there are no absolute rights or wrongs. It's your meditation practice, and feel free to experiment and find something that works for you. Dare to have fun with your practice.

If you are just starting, try using the app *Insight Timer*. It has a very good free course on learning to meditate. There are also a large number of guided meditations for almost anyone and any situation. Other apps are good - Headspace, Calm, Muse. I just turn to Insight Timer because it works for me. Bring some variety into your meditation practice.

My favorite meditation is a breathing meditation and sitting in open awareness.

Sometimes it doesn't work for me, especially if I can't sit quietly. My second favorite is walking meditation during which I focus on my steps and the flow of the world around me. When I was jogging, I even used to run as a meditation and focused on embodied awareness.

Keep a journal. I'm very undisciplined at journaling. If you saw my journals you would think of John Nash in *A Beautiful Mind*. The poems in this book came from my journal.

Use guided meditations as an easy way to get started, quiet the mind and find a meditation style that works for you. Tara Brach has a number of excellent guided meditations and teachings.

Begin or finish your meditation with short readings, either scripture or books. Thich Nhat Hanh has several short books: *Be Free Where You Are, How to Relax, How to Love*, and *Making Space* are my favorites, but he has many more.

Jon Kabat-Zinn, the founder of the Stress Reduction Clinic at the University of Massachusetts Medical School and Mindfulness-Based Stress Reduction, has a great Master Class on mindfulness and awareness. It is well worth the annual subscription to MasterClass.

Get a meditation buddy. Someone to share experiences and techniques. Hold each other accountable to your practice and inner development.

Most importantly, be kind and compassionate with yourself. You are on a grand adventure. Love yourself for having the courage to go on it.

Gibbs the Disruptor

Eight months ago, we fostered (and then adopted) a five-week-old, scared little kitten. Barbara named him "Gibbs," after

one of her favorite TV characters. Initially, the intent was he would be a playmate for our three-and-a-half-pound long-haired chihuahua, Gracie. As he's grown up (weighs almost 3 times as much as Gracie), he has become my buddy and shadow.

Gibbs quickly adapted to my morning routine. Feed the cat, make and sip coffee for a little while, and then begin my "Power Hour" - essentially reading, intentions and meditation. Gibbs does not really like that routine.

The power hour is not about sitting there doing nothing. It's play time! If I'm not paying attention to him, then he does everything he can do to get my attention. I really fought him about it. I bought toys and put him out of my study. He banged on the French doors and meowed nonstop. If I let him in, he gets into my papers and starts tearing them up - and so on. If none of that works, then he attacks my feet.

Finally, it occurred to me: You are resisting. Here's what I do now: I get his favorite toy, feathers on a stick, and hold it out in front of me as I meditate. Gibbs now floats in and out of my awareness as he plays with his toy, gets bored and walks off. And then comes back to play.

He is simply like my mind - bringing up thoughts and emotions as I sit in open awareness, become aware of the distraction and then refocus on breath. All part of the adventure into awareness and presence.

Part IV

It Takes a Community:
An Invitation

How Can We Help Each Other?

So, why doesn't everyone meditate?

Statistics show that about 14% of the people in our society meditate on an occasional or regular basis. There are hundreds of reasons why people don't meditate. Not enough time. Can't quiet the mind. Not open to it . . . and so on.

If the experiences and thoughts I've shared in this book resonate with you, I would love to hear from you. Perhaps we can share our experiences and join each other on the adventure.

If you don't have a meditation practice, or are struggling with your meditation, I would also love to hear from you. As an awareness coach, I can collaborate with you on a plan to help you through interactive guided meditations and a number of resources that are widely available.

Awareness Coaching

The Awareness Coaching Program fits very well into establishing a meditation practice.

My good friend Steve D'Annunzio, visionary and founder of Mission Driven Advisor and The Soul Purpose Institute, developed an acronym for the coaching model:

I.D.E.A.

I - Invite and investigate:
In this part program, we have an opening conversation to build trust, learn what challenges we are encountering, what our dreams and objectives are.

D - Discover and Diagnose:
We average about 60,000 thoughts a day and neuroscience has proven that we can rewire our brains and change the way we think. MindScan™ (from ProAdvisor Coach) is an assessment tool we use to scientifically measure the biases and clarity of our thoughts in six dimensions of our external and internal world, and how we think about and value in those dimensions. With this cognitive awareness we can leverage our strengths and avoid pitfalls in our professional and personal lives, relationships and activities. During this phase we imagine what change we want in our life.

E - Educate and Enroll:
We begin the investigation of meditation, its challenges, our experiences, and the benefits of a consistent practice. We begin exploring different modes of meditation.

A - Align and Activate:
We put together a customized plan with Specific, Measurable, Achievable, Relevant, Time Bound (S.M.A.R.T.) goals to develop a practice and make it an ongoing part of our life.

Awareness coaching stands on a platform of established coaching techniques and extends the practice to explore what it means to be aware by blending in both guided meditations and interactive meditations.

In a collaborative journey, we investigate the attitudinal foundations of awareness, outlined eloquently by Jon Kabat-Zinn in his master class, "Mindfulness and Meditation."

Non-judging:
We develop awareness of our judging. This doesn't mean we don't judge - the brain works that way. We instead develop the ability to be aware that we are judging

and learn to not get caught by it and become prisoners of our emotions.

Patience:
We develop an awareness of how impatient we are and release ourselves from being impatient. When we are impatient, we are pulled out of the present moment and strive for a future state.

Beginner's Mind:
We develop the ability to let go of our preconceptions and be open to the newness of reality and the world around us - eager and willing to see situations as a beginner would.

Trust:
We develop our ability to trust in our own trustworthiness, our ability to be who we are. We develop trust in our intention and our ability to be authentic and the best possible version of ourselves.

Non-striving:
We develop a deep insight into the non-dual nature of reality and understand that there is really nothing to do, no where to go and nothing to attain. This liberates us from our dualistic views of winning and losing, succeeding and failing.

Amazingly, this becomes a platform for accomplishing our goals.

Acceptance:
Acceptance is clearly seeing what reality is and from a place of wisdom choosing how we are going to engage with reality.

The real goal of an awareness practice is to extend our meditative state of awareness into the rest of our day. As we do that, we are transformed, and we transform the world around us.

We are a community

We are now in the third decade of the 21st century. We are in times of social and political strife, global sickness and catastrophic climate events. Now is the time for all of us to let go of our "optical delusion" and be one with our community, world and universe.

By helping each other meditate, we are bringing compassion, love and peace into the world.

"The greatness of a community is most accurately measured by the compassionate action of its members." - Coretta Scott King

I'm looking forward to conversation.

Bob McAuliffe
bob@outsideoftime.net

May you be peaceful
and happy, light in body
and spirit.

Many thanks to:

My loving wife and beautiful angel, Barbara, supported me through the process through reviews, editing and advice.

My daughter and master gardener, Rachael Wilmoth, took the cover photo.

My son, John C McAuliffe, MD, PhD reviewed for scientific accuracy and collaborated with me on content.

My daughter Miriam McAuliffe and son Bobby McAuliffe, and my many family members and friends who reviewed my material and encouraged me.

Carl Casanova and Ricky Russ Jr. coached me through the process of assembling and publishing.

Additional Suggested Reading:

Carl Cassanova, *What Every Successful Person Knows*, 2007, Advantage Media Group

Carlo Rovelli, *Seven Brief Lessons on Physics*, 2016, Riverhead Books, New York

Richard A. Muller, Now - *The Physics of Time*, 2016, W. W. Norton & Company, New York

Thich Nhat Hanh, *Inside the Now*, 2015, Parallax Press, Berkeley CA

Suggested Reading

Daniel J. Siegel, MD, *Aware, the Science and Practice of Presence, 2018*, NY, Penguin Random House LLC

Daniel J. Siegel, MD, Mind, *A Journey to the Heart of Being Human*, 2017, NY, W.W. Norton & Company, Inc.

Daniel Goleman & Richard J Davidson, *Altered Traits, Science Reveals How Meditation Changes Your Mind, Brain, and Body*, 2017, NY, Penguin Random House LLC

Elizabeth Blackburn, PhD & Elissa Epel, PhD, *The Telomere Effect*, 2017, NY, Grand Central Publishing

Dawson Church, Bliss Brain, *the Neuroscience of Remodeling Your Brain for Resilience, Creativity, and Joy*, 2020, Hay House, Inc. 12

Steve D'Annunzio, *The New Prosperity Paradigm*, coming in 2021.

Sean Carroll, *Something Deeply Hidden, Quantum Worlds and the Emergence of Spacetime*, 2019, Penguin Random House LLC

George Musser, *Spooky Action at a Distance, the Phenomenon That Reimagines Space and Time*, 2015, New York, Scientific American / Farrar, Straus and Giroux

"It has been an honor to work with Bob for these past few years! Bob's commitment to his Mission of bringing more Compassion, Peace and Love into the world is beautiful to witness. His kind heart, fun sense of humor, generous spirit, creative abilities and caring nature are what draw me to confidently support his coaching practice of helping folks build and sustain their meditation skills and disciplines. I am so grateful that there are people like him in the world! I encourage you to connect with Bob if you are interested in receiving mentorship in your meditation practice!"

- Raeanne Lacatena,
Holistic Business Coach and Counselor

"At last... a meditation book combining the scientific and spiritual aspects of the power and value of meditation. Using prose and poetry, Bob gives the reader both the medical and magical means to achieve mindfulness and increase inner peace."

- Steve D'Annunzio, CPC
CEO-Mission Driven Advisor
Soul Purpose Institute

"Every once in a while, you encounter someone who makes you pause, reflect, redirect...a person who speaks calmly and quietly but their words ring more boldly than most around you. Bob has been one of those people for me. He has been helping me to approach my personal life, my business and myself with a renewed understanding and awareness. Bob is an insightful coach and mentor and has become a calming, loving and uplifting presence in my life. Through discussion, reflection, and meditation with Bob, I've gained clarity around my goals and am developing a more peaceful acceptance of my place and purpose in life."

- Tara Wilson
Eventsia Group

"Just reading this book, my breath deepened, my heart rate slowed, my mind both stilled and expanded; the poems took me on a journey of "clsc", there is no way to describe it. The science behind meditation, wrapped in tales of discovery, leads us to a place where we can't help but want to try it."

- Mary R. Parker, CPC
MRP Coaching LLC